Mother Teresa

Walking with Her Saints

edited by
Hiroshi Katayanagi, SJ

Paulist Press
New York/Mahwah, NJ

Caseside design by Cynthia Dunne
Book design by Lynn Else

Library of Congress Cataloging-in-Publication Data

Mother Teresa : walking with her saints / edited by Hiroshi Katayanagi.
    p. cm.
  ISBN 978-0-8091-0576-2 (alk. paper)
  1. Christian saints—Quotations. 2. Christian saints—Pictorial works. 3. Teresa, Mother, 1910–1997—Quotations. 4. Teresa, Mother, 1910–1997—Pictorial works. 5. Bible—Quotations. 6. Devotional literature. I. Katayanagi, Hiroshi.
  BX4655.3.M68 2007
  282.092′2—dc22

                                2006035344

Published by Paulist Press
997 Macarthur Boulevard
Mahwah, New Jersey 07430

www.paulistpress.com

Printed and bound in the United States of America

Contents

Preface

It is with great honor and devotion that we offer our readers this inspiring sequel to *My Dear Children*, which has been so popularly received in recent years.

In *Mother Teresa: Walking with Her Saints* you will find a superb collection of selected quotes from various saints, many from our own Paulist library of books, accompanied by stunning photographs taken by Hiroshi Katayanagi, who walked alongside Mother Teresa before joining the Society of Jesus. Combined, they are a testament to the holiness and wisdom that Mother Teresa shares with the communion saints who were her companions and inspiration along her journey.

It is my hope that you, too, will be inspired not just by the images of Mother Teresa, but also by the words uttered by the saints in this book. As you read *Mother Teresa: Walking with Her Saints*, may you be nourished along your own journey toward God, the giver of all life and goodness.

Lawrence Boadt, CSP
Publisher

Introduction

The church is like a harmony played by different instruments. It may surprise us that a variety of charisms and spiritualities can flow together to produce the church's one mystical harmony. But there is no doubt that Mother Teresa was one of the outstanding musicians in this harmony of charisms. We see in her words and deeds the echoes of saints such as Francis of Assisi, Ignatius of Loyola, St. Thérèse of Lisieux, and Mother Cabrini, as well as of holy men and women like Mary Ward and Thomas à Kempis.

In childhood, Mother Teresa was inspired by the life of Francis of Assisi. She dreamed of dedicating herself to the poor and living a life of poverty. While still in high school, she read letters written by Jesuit missionaries working in India and heard the call to become a missionary herself. A Jesuit priest advised her to join the Loreto Sisters, who had been founded by Mary Ward based on the spirituality of Ignatius of Loyola. In 1918, Mother Teresa went to Ireland, the land of St. Patrick, to study the spirituality of the Loreto Sisters. She took the name Teresa out of a desire to live an inconspicuous, simple life of service to God following the model of St. Thérèse of Lisieux. Some months later she boarded a ship to India.

After eighteen years with the Loreto Sisters in India, she heard a mystical voice prompting her to go out from her convent to serve the poor, suffering, and dying in the gutters of Calcutta. While she was reflecting and praying over this possibility, she read the biography of Mother Cabrini, an Italian religious sister who went to the United States to serve poor immigrants. Mother Teresa then asked herself if she could do for the Indian people what Mother Cabrini did for the poor in America. Her superiors judged her vocation to be genuine, and she received permission to work outside the convent as a religious sister. Mother Teresa started her work for the poor in 1948, when she was thirty-eight years old. Throughout her ministry, she was guided by the saints and *The Imitation of Christ* by Thomas à Kempis, which itself had so deeply influenced Ignatius of Loyola, Mary Ward, and St. Thérèse of Lisieux.

In this small book I have gathered the words and prayers of saints who were dear to Mother Teresa so that you might experience the harmony of the church that resonated throughout her life. Each word or prayer is joined with a quotation from the Bible. For the scriptures empowered and enlightened Mother Teresa as they have all the church's saints, bringing them closer to God, the conductor of this harmony of charisms that make up the church.

Hiroshi Katayanagi, SJ

Mother Teresa

Walking with Her Saints

Strength

O Divine Master, grant that
I may not so much seek to be consoled
as to console, to be understood as to understand,
to be loved as to love.
Prayer of St. Francis

Peace I leave with you; my peace I give to you.
I do not give to you as the world gives.
Do not let your hearts be troubled,
and do not let them be afraid.
John 14:27

Holiness

"We are not social workers…[but] contemplatives in the heart of the world. For we are touching the Body of Christ twenty-four hours a day."

Mother Teresa

The grass withers, and the flower falls, but the word of the Lord endures forever.

1 Peter 1:24–25

Communion

Show yourselves at all times glad and joyful,
for Almighty God loves a cheerful giver.

Mary Ward

Now the whole group of those who believed were
of one heart and soul, and no one claimed private
ownership of any possessions, but everything
they owned was held in common.

Acts 4:32

MOTHER

Compassion

Never seek to fly from that which our
Savior so willingly embraced.

Mary Ward

Can a woman forget her nursing child,
or show no compassion for the child of her womb?
Even these may forget, yet I will not forget you.

Isaiah 49:15

Inspiration

For God it is not the possible we should do,
but the impossible.
St. Frances Xavier Cabrini

To you I lift up my eyes,
O you who are enthroned in the heavens!
Psalm 123:1

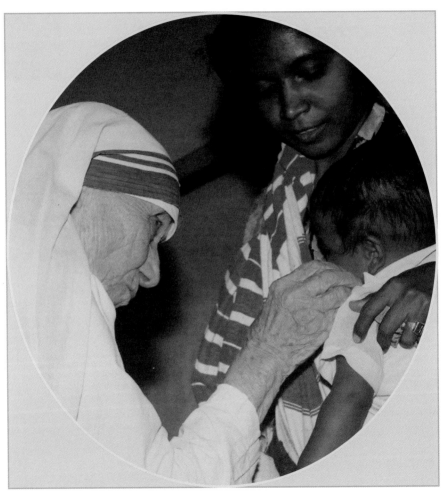

Love

Why did you so dignify us?
With unimaginable love you looked upon your creatures
within your very self, and you fell in love with us.
St. Catherine of Siena

But Jesus said, "Let the little children come to me,
and do not stop them; for it is to such as these that the
kingdom of heaven belongs." And he laid his hands on
them and went on his way.
Matthew 19:14–15

Calling

We shall weave a chain of love around the world.

Mother Teresa

The Spirit of the Lord is upon me, because he has
anointed me to bring good news to the poor.
He has sent me to proclaim release to the captives
and recovery of sight to the blind,
to let the oppressed go free.

Luke 4:18

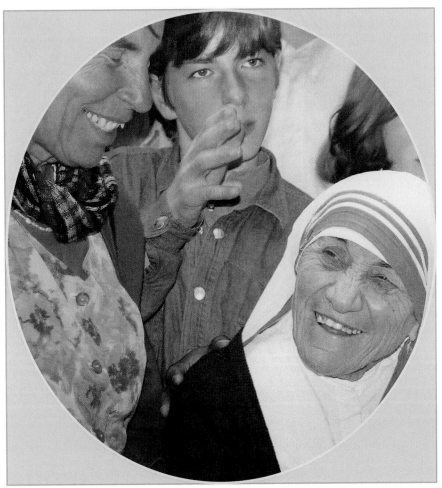

Fellowship

And be certain that the more advanced you see you are
in love for your neighbor the more advanced
you will be in the love of God.

St. Teresa of Avila

The commandment we have from him is this:
those who love God must love their
brothers and sisters also.

1 John 4:21

Integrity

"…when I visited Calcutta I saw an unknown woman,
vigorous and purposeful, feeding and caring for
skeletonized human beings….So I asked the nun,
whom they called Mother Teresa, and she told me,
'…each one is Jesus in a distressing disguise.'
We became life-long friends from that day."
Dorothy Day

The righteous walk in integrity—
happy are the children who follow them!
Proverbs 20:7

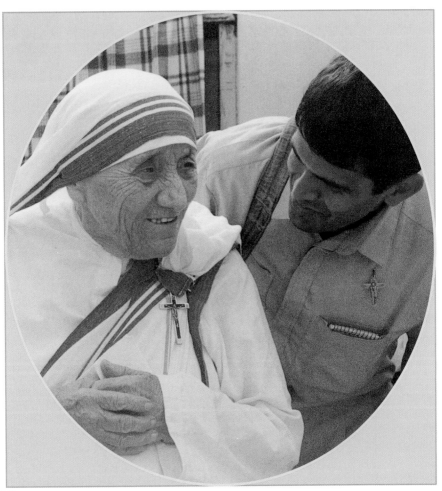

Mercy

Keep the joy of loving God always in your heart and
share this joy with all you meet.

Mother Teresa

"Which of these three, do you think, was a neighbor to
the man who fell into the hands of the robbers?"
He said, "The one who showed him mercy."
Jesus said to him, "Go and do likewise."

Luke 10:36–37

Faith

Most High, glorious God,
enlighten the shadows of my heart,
and grant unto me a right faith,
a certain hope and perfect charity,
sense and understanding…

St. Francis of Assisi's Prayer before a Crucifix

Rejoice always. Pray without ceasing.

1 Thessalonians 5:16–17

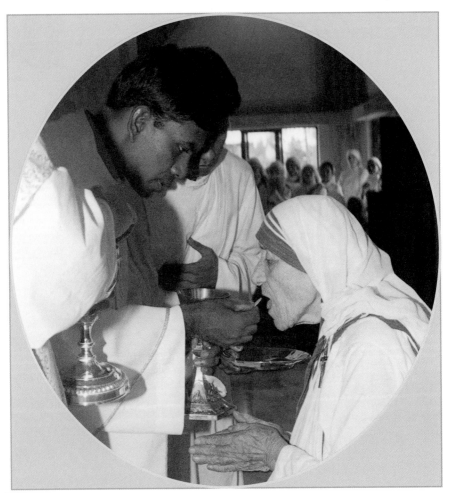

Praise

O how I love Jesus, who comes in the Host to unite
Himself to my enraptured soul.

St. Thérèse of Lisieux

Then I will go to the altar of God,
to God my exceeding joy;
and I will praise you with the harp,
O God, my God.

Psalm 43:4

Witness

Make me preach to you without preaching,
not by words but by my example.

John Henry Newman

You yourselves are our letter, written on our hearts,
to be known and read by all.

2 Corinthians 3:2

Charity

You can save only one at a time.

We can love only one at a time.

Mother Teresa

And the king will answer them, "Truly I tell you,
just as you did it to one of the least of these who are
members of my family, you did it to me."

Matthew 25:40

Faithfulness

We are called upon not to be successful
but to be faithful.

Mother Teresa

Here is a call for the endurance of the saints,
those who keep the commandments of God
and hold fast to the faith of Jesus.

Revelation 14:12

Prayer

Prayer is a cry of gratitude and love,
in the midst of trial as well as in joy.
St. Thérèse of Lisieux

Your prayers and your alms have ascended
as a memorial before God.
Acts 10:4

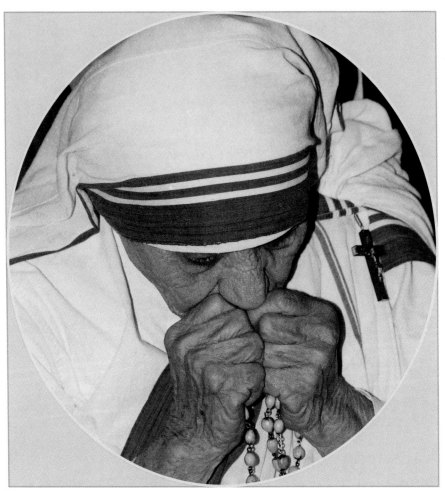

Mary

I do not tremble when I see my weakness, for the
treasures of a mother belong also to her child,
and I am your child, O dear Mother Mary.
St. Thérèse of Lisieux

But Mary treasured all these words and
pondered them in her heart.
Luke 2:19

Wisdom

Look upon us, eternal Son of God, who took flesh in the
womb of the Virgin Mary! All humanity, with its burden
of trials and troubles, stands in need of you.

Pope John Paul II

For wisdom becomes known through speech, and
education through the words of the tongue.

Sirach 4:24

Service

Make us worthy, Lord,
To serve our fellow men throughout the world
who live and die in poverty and hunger.
Pope Paul VI

For you have been a refuge to the poor,
a refuge to the needy in their distress,
a shelter from the rainstorm and
a shade from the heat.
Isaiah 25:4

Surrender

Take, O Lord, and receive
All my liberty, my memory, my understanding,
And my entire will.
Whatever I have or hold, you have given me.
I restore it all to you and surrender it wholly
To be governed by your will.

St. Ignatius of Loyola

To you, O Lord, I lift up my soul.

Psalm 25:1

Humility

O Jesus! Meek and humble of heart, Hear me.
From the desire of being esteemed, Deliver me, Jesus.
From the desire of being loved…
From the desire of being extolled…
From the desire of being honored…
From the desire of being praised…
From the Litany of Humility

For where two or three are gathered in my name, I am there among them.
Matthew 18:20

Generosity

Teach us, Good Lord,
to serve you as you deserve;
to give and not count the cost;
to fight and not heed the wounds;
to toil and not seek for rest;
to labor and not ask for reward,
except knowing that we do your will.
Amen.

St. Ignatius of Loyola

Since there will never cease to be some in need on the earth, I therefore command you, "Open your hand to the poor and needy neighbor in your land."

Deuteronomy 15:11

Grace

Have you learned to pray yet?…Once you have found
God, it is up to you to do with Him as you wish.

Mother Teresa

I will turn their mourning into joy,
I will comfort them, and give them gladness for sorrow.

Jeremiah 31:13

Salvation

The cry of Jesus on the Cross, "I thirst" (John 19:28),
expressing the depth of God's longing for man, penetrated
Mother Teresa's soul and found fertile soil in her heart.
Satiating Jesus' thirst for love and for souls in union
with Mary, the Mother of Jesus, had become the sole aim
of Mother Teresa's existence and the inner force
that drew her out of herself and made her "run in haste"
across the globe to labor for the salvation and the
sanctification of the poorest of the poor.

Pope John Paul II

After this, when Jesus knew that all was now finished,
he said (in order to fulfill the scripture), "I am thirsty."

John 19:28

Peace

So I saw that God is our true peace; and he is our safe
protector when we ourselves are in disquiet, and he
constantly works to bring us into endless peace.
Julian of Norwich

By contrast, the fruit of the Spirit is love, joy, peace,
patience, kindness, generosity, faithfulness.
Galatians 5:22

Suffering

At the end of his life, stripped naked, scourged at the pillar, parched with thirst, he was so poor on the wood of the cross that neither the earth nor the wood could give him a place to lay his head. He had nowhere to rest it except upon his own shoulder.

St. Catherine of Siena

She opens her hand to the poor, and reaches out her hands to the needy.

Proverbs 31:20

Selflessness

He who has true and perfect charity seeks self in nothing,
but searches all things for the glory of God.
Thomas à Kempis

For all of them have contributed out of their abundance;
but she out of her poverty has put in everything
she had, all she had to live on.
Mark 12:44

Devotion

I saw very truly that all our endless friendship, our place,
our life, and our being are in God.

Julian of Norwich

"…I considered these things inwardly, and pondered in
my heart that in kinship with wisdom there is immortality,
and in friendship with her, pure delight, and in the
labors of her hands, unfailing wealth, and in the
experience of her company, understanding,
and renown in sharing her words."

Wisdom 8:17—18

Peacemakers

It does no harm to esteem yourself less than anyone else, but it is very harmful to think yourself better than even one. The humble live in continuous peace, while in the hearts of the proud are envy and frequent anger.

Thomas à Kempis

"Blessed are the peacemakers, for they will be called children of God."

Matthew 5:9

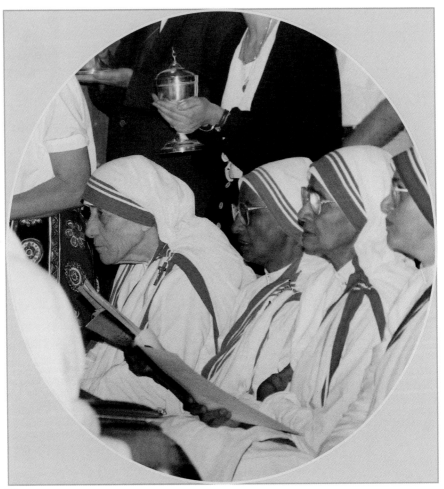

Sanctity

Soul of Christ, sanctify me,
Body of Christ, save me,
Blood of Christ, inebriate me,
Water from the side of Christ, wash me,
Passion of Christ, strengthen me.

Anima Christi

Do not work for the food that perishes,
but for the food that endures for eternal life,
which the Son of Man will give you. For it is on him
that God the Father has set his seal.

John 6:27

Magnificat

Prayer is anything that elevates, anything supernatural
that enlarges the soul and unites it to God.

St. Thérèse of Lisieux

And Mary said, "My soul magnifies the Lord,
and my spirit rejoices in God my Savior."

Luke 1:46–47

Sources

Strength
St. Francis of Assisi, the Prayers, http://www.san-francesco.org/preghiere_eng.html.

Holiness
Robert Ellsberg, *All Saints: Daily Reflections on Saints, Prophets, and Witnesses for Our Time,* (New York: Crossroad Publishing, 1997), 393.

Communion
M. Pauline Parker, IBVM, *The Spirit of Mary Ward* (London: Thomas More Books Ltd., 1963), 86.

Compassion
The Institute of the Blessed Virgin Mary, ed., *The Mind and Maxims of Mary Ward,* Paternoster Series: no. 17 (London: Burns, Oates & Washbourne, Ltd., 1959).

Inspiration
Sue Stanton, *Great Women of Faith* (Mahwah, NJ: Paulist Press, 2003), 10.

Love

Suzanne Noffke, OP, trans. and ed., *Catherine of Siena—The Dialogue*, Classics of Western Spirituality (Mahwah, NJ: Paulist Press, 1980), 49.

Calling

Elaine Murray Stone, *Mother Teresa: A Life of Love*, (Mahwah, NJ: Paulist Press, 1999), 105.

Fellowship

Kieran Kavanaugh, OCD, and Otilio Rodriguez, OCD, trans. and ed., *Teresa of Avila—The Interior Castle*, Classics of Western Spirituality (Mahwah, NJ: Paulist Press, 1979), 100.

Integrity

Richard Leonard, SJ, *Preaching to the Converted* (Mahwah, NJ: Paulist Press, 2006).

Mercy

From a letter from Mother Teresa to *Frontline: India's National Magazine* on October 1993. Letter included by Navin Chawla in *Frontline*, October 3, 1997.

Faith

St. Francis of Assisi, the Prayers (http://www.san-francesco.org/preghiere_eng.html)

Praise
Thérèse of Lisieux, *The Little Way for Every Day—Thoughts from Thérèse of Lisieux*, selected and translated by Francis Broome, CSP (Mahwah, NJ: Paulist Press, 2006), 35.

Witness
John Henry Newman, *Prayers, Verses, and Devotion* (San Francisco: Ignatius Press, 1989), 389.

Charity
Robert Ellsberg, *All Saints: Daily Reflections on Saints, Prophets, and Witnesses for Our Time*, (New York: Crossroad Publishing, 1997), 394.

Faithfulness
Navin Chawla, *Frontline: India's National Magazine*, October 3, 1997.

Prayer
Thérèse of Lisieux, *The Little Way for Every Day—Thoughts from Thérèse of Lisieux*, selected and translated by Francis Broome, CSP (Mahwah, NJ: Paulist Press, 2006), 45.

Mary
Thérèse of Lisieux, *The Little Way for Every Day—Thoughts from Thérèse of Lisieux*, selected and translated by Francis Broome, CSP (Mahwah, NJ: Paulist Press, 2006), 9.

Wisdom
Homily of Pope John Paul II on Christmas Eve, 2004, in Walter J. Ziemba, *Pope John Paul II—Reflections on the Man* (Mahwah, NJ: Paulist Press, 2005), 9.

Service
Pope Paul VI, http://www.catholic.org/clife/prayers/prayer.php?p=194.

Surrender
St. Ignatius of Loyola, http://www.companysj.com/v161/discernm.html.

Humility
From the "Litany of Humility," by Cardinal Merry del Val, from the *Jesuit Prayer Book*, 1963. (http://www.ewtn.com/devotionals/Litanies/humility.htm).

Generosity
Prayer of Ignatius Loyola (http://www.prayerfoundation.org/prayer_of_ignatius_of_loyola.htm).

Grace
Navin Chawla, *Frontline: India's National Magazine*, October 3, 1997.

Salvation
Homily of Pope John Paul II at the Beatification of Mother Teresa, October 19, 2003. (From the Vatican Web site)

Peace
Edmund Colledge, OSA, and James Walsh, SJ, trans. and ed., *Julian of Norwich—Showings*, Classics of Western Spirituality (Mahwah, NJ: Paulist Press, 1978), 265.

Suffering
Suzanne Noffke, OP, trans. and ed., *Catherine of Siena—The Dialogue*, Classics of Western Spirituality (Mahwah, NJ: Paulist Press, 1980), 320.

Selflessness
Thomas à Kempis, *The Imitation of Christ*, bk. 1, chap. 15, trans. Aloysius Croft, Harold Bolton (Mineola, NY: Dover Publications, 2003).

Devotion
Mary E. Penrose, *Refreshing Water from Ancient Wells* (Mahwah, NJ: Paulist Press, 2004), 87.

Peacemakers
Thomas à Kempis, *The Imitation of Christ*, bk. 1, chap. 7, trans. Aloysius Croft, Harold Bolton (Mineola, NY: Dover Publications, 2003).

Sanctity
Traditional.

Magnificat
Thérèse of Lisieux, *The Little Way for Every Day—Thoughts from Thérèse of Lisieux*, selected and translated by Francis Broome, CSP (Mahwah, NJ: Paulist Press, 2006), 45.

Photo Captions

Cover: January 6, 1995, in the courtyard of the motherhouse in Calcutta.

[Page 2] December 7, 1994, in the courtyard of the motherhouse where Mother is blessing her sisters who have taken their final vows.

[Page 4] November 20, 1994, on the grounds of St. Xavier College in Calcutta.

[Page 6] November 27, 1995. Singing with newly vowed sisters in the courtyard of the motherhouse.

[Page 8] May 19, 1995, at St. Mary's Church in Calcutta before the first vows.

[Page 10] January 6, 1995, in the courtyard of the motherhouse.

[Page 12] May 19, 1995, at St. Mary's Church before the first vows.

[Page 14] December 8, 1994, at St. Mary's Church. Sisters, who have taken their first vows, are wearing the cross given by Mother.

[Page 16] January 6, 1995, in the courtyard of the motherhouse.

[Page 18] August 26, 1995, in the courtyard of the motherhouse on Mother's eighty-fifth birthday.

[Page 20] November 12, 1995, at the "House of Children" in Calcutta.

[Page 22] October 22, 1995, at a chapel in the motherhouse.

[Page 24] October 21, 1995, at an ordination Mass in Calcutta.

[Page 26] December 7, 1994, at St. Mary's Church before the final vows.

[Page 28] December 25, 1994, at a home for sick and dying poor in Calcutta.

[Page 30] December 7, 1994, at St. Mary's Church in Calcutta.

[Page 32] October 21, 1995, at an ordination Mass in Calcutta.

[Page 34] December 7, 1994, at St. Mary's Church before final vows.

[Page 36] November 27, 1994, in the courtyard of the motherhouse. Mother is talking to one of her sisters who have just taken their final vows.

[Page 38] Laundry drying on the roof of a home for sick and dying poor. The building behind the roof is a famous Hindu Temple of Kali.

[Page 40] January 6, 1995, in the courtyard of the motherhouse.